Teach Your Child to Read

300 Short Easy Sentences

English - Norwegian

Name 

I Can...

- [ ] read the 1st sentence.
- [ ] read the 2nd sentence.
- [ ] make a sentence from a picture.
- [ ] color a picture.
- [ ] Draw a picture.

The frog is going to a party.

Frosken skal på fest.

The happy frog is wearing a green hat.

Den glade frosken har på seg en grønn hatt.

Name ____________________

I Can...

- ☐ read the 1st sentence.
- ☐ read the 2nd sentence.
- ☐ make a sentence from a picture.
- ☐ color a picture.
- ☐ Draw a picture.

Owl likes to read big books.

Uglen liker å lese store bøker.

A smart owl is reading an alphabet book.

En smart ugle leser en alfabetbok.

I Can...

- [ ] read the 1st sentence.
- [ ] read the 2nd sentence.
- [ ] make a sentence from a picture.
- [ ] color a picture.
- [ ] Draw a picture.

Come on! The ice cream truck is here!

Kom igjen! Isbilen er her!

He is driving a big icecream truck.

Han kjører en stor isbil.

I Can...

- [ ] read the 1st sentence.
- [ ] read the 2nd sentence.
- [ ] make a sentence from a picture.
- [ ] color a picture.
- [ ] Draw a picture.

Dragons are very friendly and have scales on their backs.

Drager er veldig vennlige og har vekter på ryggen.

The dragon is waving his hand.

Dragen vifter med hånden.

Name

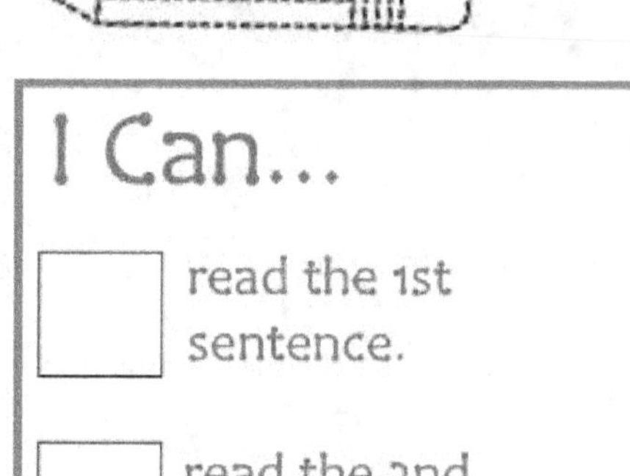

I Can...

- [ ] read the 1st sentence.
- [ ] read the 2nd sentence.
- [ ] make a sentence from a picture.
- [ ] color a picture.
- [ ] Draw a picture.

This ram lives in the farmhouse.

Denne rammen bor i våningshuset.

Ram has a large horn and fluffy wool.

Ram har et stort horn og myk ull.

Name

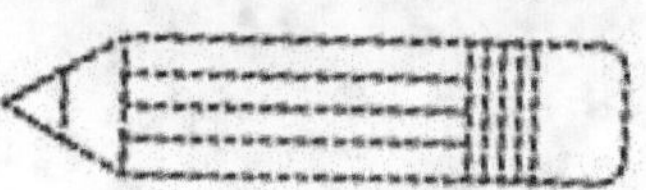

I Can...

- ☐ read the 1st sentence.
- ☐ read the 2nd sentence.
- ☐ make a sentence from a picture.
- ☐ color a picture.
- ☐ Draw a picture.

The bunny likes to eat carrots.

Bunny liker á spise gulrøtter.

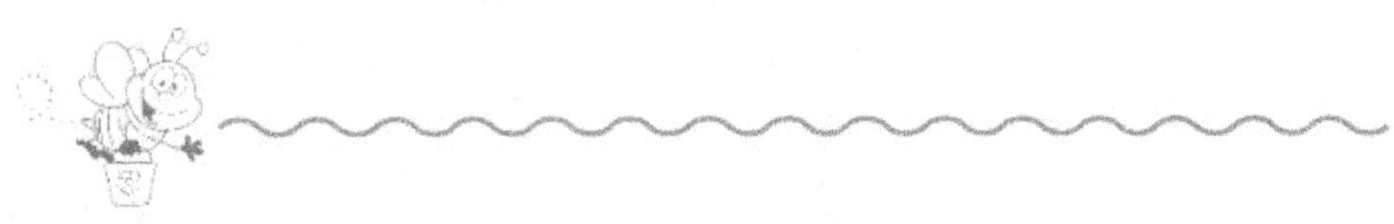

Rabbit thinks that the juicy orange carrot looks yummy.

Kanin synes at den saftige oransje gulroten ser yummy ut.

Name _______________________ 

I Can...

- [ ] read the 1st sentence.
- [ ] read the 2nd sentence.
- [ ] make a sentence from a picture.
- [ ] color a picture.
- [ ] Draw a picture.

The clown likes to give out balloons to little kids.

Klovnen liker å gi ut ballonger til små barn.

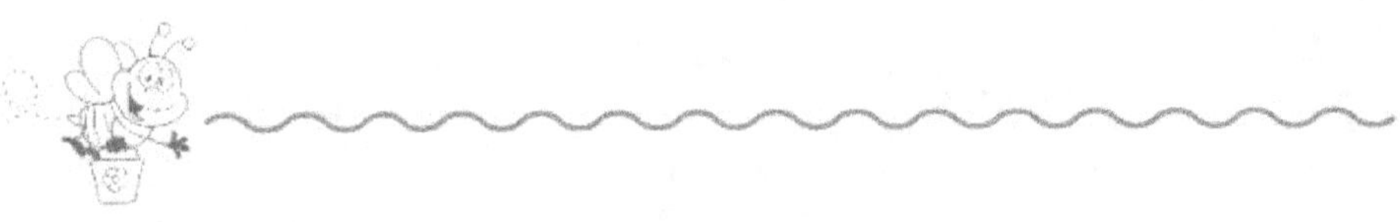

Funny, Mr. Clown is giving away colorful balloons.

Morsomt, Mr. Clown gir bort fargerike ballonger.

Name

I Can...

- [ ] read the 1st sentence.
- [ ] read the 2nd sentence.
- [ ] make a sentence from a picture.
- [ ] color a picture.
- [ ] Draw a picture.

The clown is juggling balls for his performance.

Klovnen sjonglerer baller for sin prestasjon.

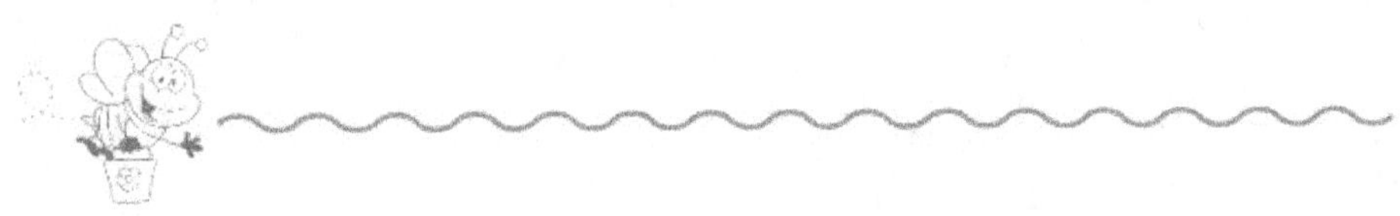

Talented, Mr. Clown is juggling five red balls.

Mr. talentfull, sjonglerer fem røde baller.

Name

I Can...

- [ ] read the 1st sentence.
- [ ] read the 2nd sentence.
- [ ] make a sentence from a picture.
- [ ] color a picture.
- [ ] Draw a picture.

The Easter Bunny is going to give out chocolate eggs.

Påskeharen kommer til å gi ut sjokoladeegg.

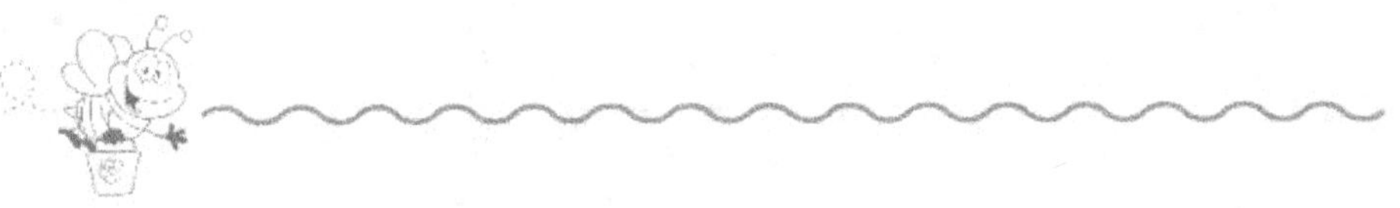

The rabbit goes out to buy more orange carrots.

Kaninen går ut for å kjøpe mer oransje gulrøtter.

Name

I Can...

- [ ] read the 1st sentence.
- [ ] read the 2nd sentence.
- [ ] make a sentence from a picture.
- [ ] color a picture.
- [ ] Draw a picture.

The pencil is drawing a zig-zag line.

Blyanten tegner en sikksakk-linje.

The Pencil is saying hello to you.

Blyanten sier hei til deg.

Name 

I Can...

- [ ] read the 1st sentence.
- [ ] read the 2nd sentence.
- [ ] make a sentence from a picture.
- [ ] color a picture.
- [ ] Draw a picture.

The pencil put on a big smile and went to work.

Blyanten la på seg et stort smil og gikk på jobb.

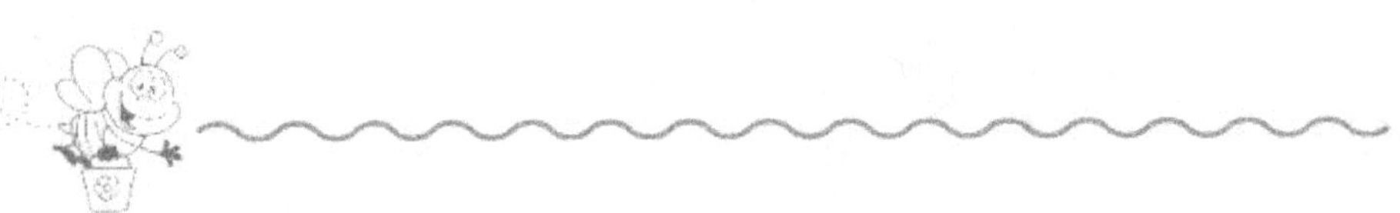

The Pencil is leaving to go on a long relaxing vacation.

Blyanten drar for å dra på en lang avslappende ferie.

Name _______________________

I Can...

- [ ] read the 1st sentence.
- [ ] read the 2nd sentence.
- [ ] make a sentence from a picture.
- [ ] color a picture.
- [ ] Draw a picture.

This snowman is my friend, and he is a helper of Santa.

Denne snømannen er min venn, og han er en hjelper til julenissen.

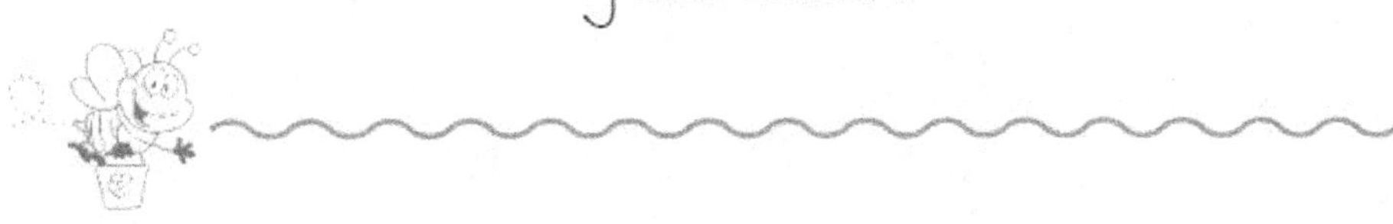

Mr. Snowman is celebrating Christmas by the decorated tree.

Mr. Snowman feirer jul av det dekorerte treet.

Name 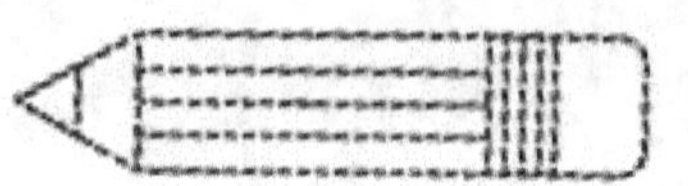

I Can...

- [ ] read the 1st sentence.
- [ ] read the 2nd sentence.
- [ ] make a sentence from a picture.
- [ ] color a picture.
- [ ] Draw a picture.

The octopus is working as a chef and serving food.

Blekkspruten jobber som kokk og serverer mat.

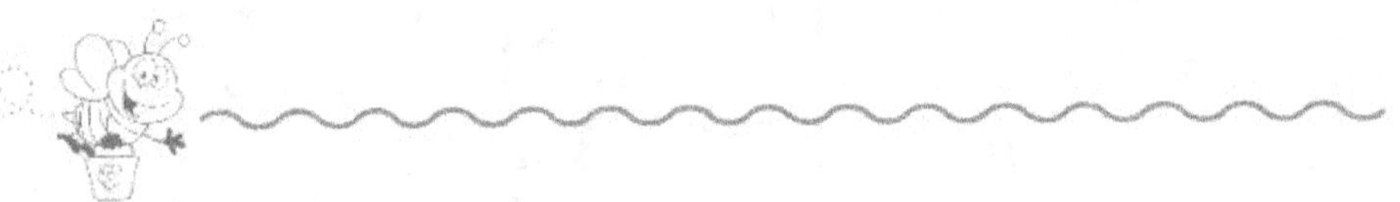

Chef Octopus is serving a delicious turkey dinner.

Chef Octopus serverer en deilig kalkunmiddag.

Name

I Can...

- [ ] read the 1st sentence.
- [ ] read the 2nd sentence.
- [ ] make a sentence from a picture.
- [ ] color a picture.
- [ ] Draw a picture.

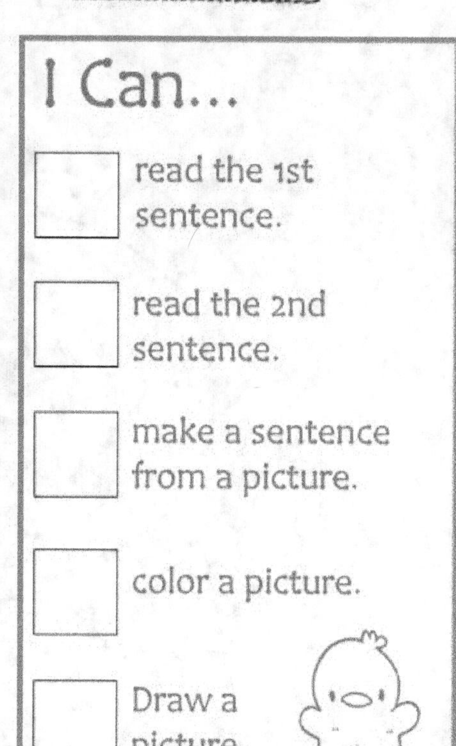

Santa is happy.

Julenissen er fornøyd.

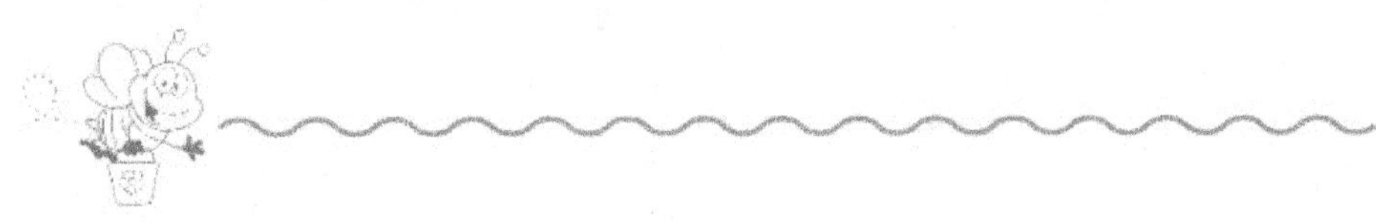

Santa Claus is giving extraordinary presents to excited kids.

Julenissen gir ekstraordinære gaver til spente barn.

Name

I Can...

- [ ] read the 1st sentence.
- [ ] read the 2nd sentence.
- [ ] make a sentence from a picture.
- [ ] color a picture.
- [ ] Draw a picture.

The bear likes to eat sweets.

Bjørnen spiser søtsaker.

Teddy is licking a red and white candy cane.

Teddy slikker en rød og hvit sukkerrør.

Name ____________________

I Can...

- ☐ read the 1st sentence.
- ☐ read the 2nd sentence.
- ☐ make a sentence from a picture.
- ☐ color a picture.
- ☐ Draw a picture.

The book has a wand.

Boken har et tryllestav.

~~~~~~~~~~~~~~~~~~~~~~~~~

The cereal box got a magician set for Christmas.

Frokostblandingsboksen fikk en tryllekunstner til jul.
~~~~~~~~~~~~~~~~~~~~~~~~~

Name

I Can...

- [ ] read the 1st sentence.
- [ ] read the 2nd sentence.
- [ ] make a sentence from a picture.
- [ ] color a picture.
- [ ] Draw a picture.

The bear has a present.

Bjørnen har en gave.

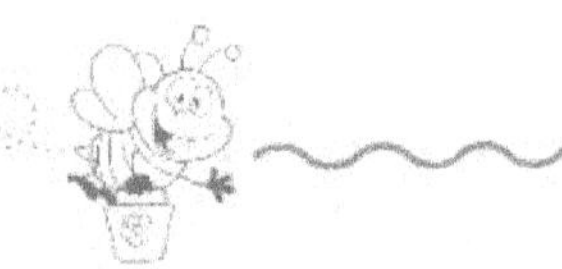

Happy Teddy is opening his box of presents from Santa.

Happy Teddy åpner sin eske med gaver fra julenissen.

Name _________________________ 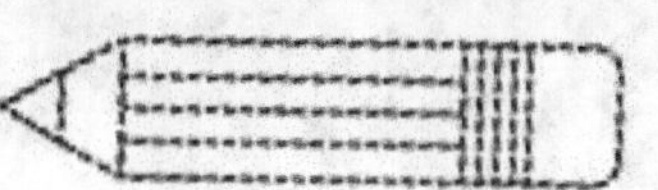

I Can...

- [ ] read the 1st sentence.
- [ ] read the 2nd sentence.
- [ ] make a sentence from a picture.
- [ ] color a picture.
- [ ] Draw a picture.

Santa is going to give out presents.

Julenissen kommer til å gi gaver.

Santa is lugging a large brown bag of gifts to his sley.

Julenissen holder på med en stor brun pose med gaver til selen.

Name

I Can...

- [ ] read the 1st sentence.
- [ ] read the 2nd sentence.
- [ ] make a sentence from a picture.
- [ ] color a picture.
- [ ] Draw a picture.

I made a snowman.

Jeg laget en snømann.

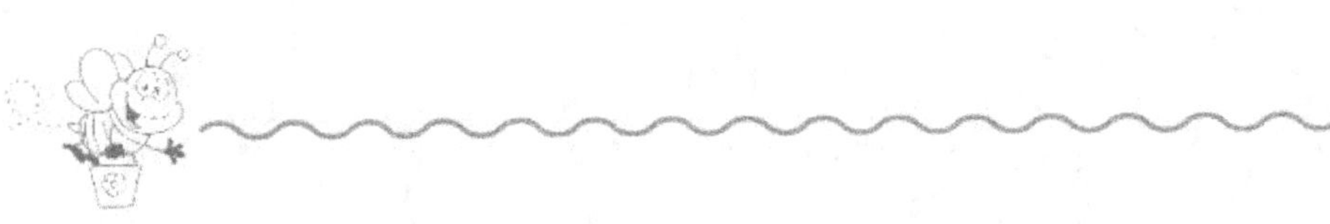

Mr. Snowman is holding a broom and saying goodbye.

Mr. Snowman holder en kost og sier farvel.

I Can...

- [ ] read the 1st sentence.
- [ ] read the 2nd sentence.
- [ ] make a sentence from a picture.
- [ ] color a picture.
- [ ] Draw a picture.

The parrot is colorful.

Papegøyen er fargerik.

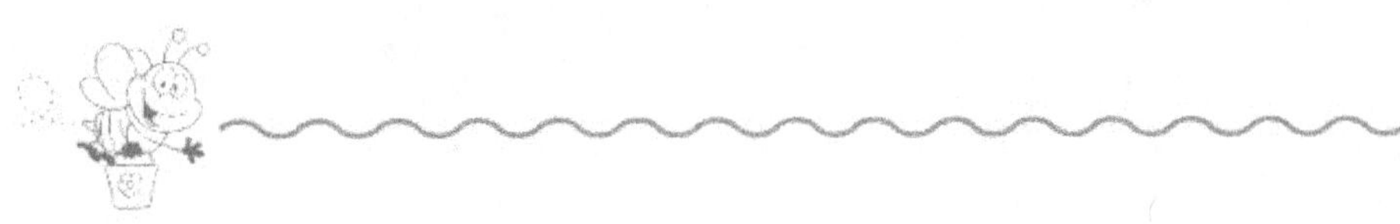

The green parrot came from the forest to the zoo.

Den grønne papegøyen kom fra skogen til dyrehagen.

Name

I Can...

- [ ] read the 1st sentence.
- [ ] read the 2nd sentence.
- [ ] make a sentence from a picture.
- [ ] color a picture.
- [ ] Draw a picture.

There are a lot of animals.

Det er mange dyr.

The animals are happy being together again.

Dyrene er glade for å være sammen igjen.

Name

I Can...

- [ ] read the 1st sentence.
- [ ] read the 2nd sentence.
- [ ] make a sentence from a picture.
- [ ] color a picture.
- [ ] Draw a picture.

The man is wearing a belt.

Mannen har belte på seg.

The carpenter is fixing something.

Tømreren fikser noe.

Name

I Can...

- [ ] read the 1st sentence.
- [ ] read the 2nd sentence.
- [ ] make a sentence from a picture.
- [ ] color a picture.
- [ ] Draw a picture.

The rabbit is very young.

Kaninen er veldig ung.

The magician plays a trick.

Trollmannen spiller et triks.

Name

I Can...

- [ ] read the 1st sentence.
- [ ] read the 2nd sentence.
- [ ] make a sentence from a picture.
- [ ] color a picture.
- [ ] Draw a picture.

He has a potion.

Han har en potion.

The scientist is making a potion.

Forskeren lager en potion.

Name 

I Can...

- [ ] read the 1st sentence.
- [ ] read the 2nd sentence.
- [ ] make a sentence from a picture.
- [ ] color a picture.
- [ ] Draw a picture.

He is wearing sunglasses.

Han har på seg solbriller.

The policeman is mad.

Politimannen er sint.

Name

I Can...

- [ ] read the 1st sentence.
- [ ] read the 2nd sentence.
- [ ] make a sentence from a picture.
- [ ] color a picture.
- [ ] Draw a picture.

He has a bucket of paint.

Han har en bøtte med maling.

He likes to paint.

Han liker å male.

Name

I Can...

- ☐ read the 1st sentence.
- ☐ read the 2nd sentence.
- ☐ make a sentence from a picture.
- ☐ color a picture.
- ☐ Draw a picture.

The man has a hat.

Mannen har hatt.

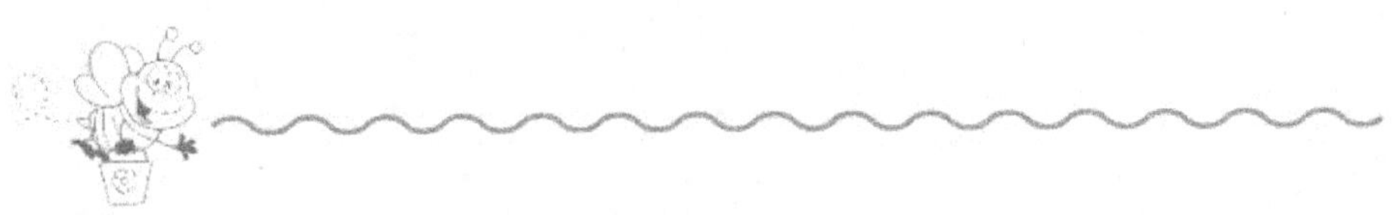

The postman is giving out the mail in the early morning.

Postmannen gir ut posten tidlig på morgenen.

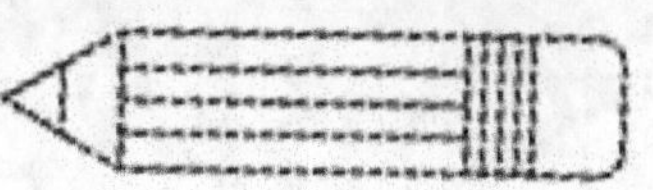

28

I Can...

- ☐ read the 1st sentence.
- ☐ read the 2nd sentence.
- ☐ make a sentence from a picture.
- ☐ color a picture.
- ☐ Draw a picture.

He has a walkie talkie.

Han har en walkie talkie.

He is going to work with his suitcase.

Han skal jobbe med kofferten.

Name

I Can...

- [ ] read the 1st sentence.
- [ ] read the 2nd sentence.
- [ ] make a sentence from a picture.
- [ ] color a picture.
- [ ] Draw a picture.

He is sleepy.

Han er søvnig.

The delivery man sent us a package.

Leveringsmannen sendte oss en pakke.

Name

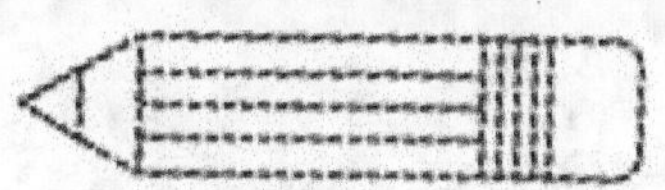

I Can...

- [ ] read the 1st sentence.
- [ ] read the 2nd sentence.
- [ ] make a sentence from a picture.
- [ ] color a picture.
- [ ] Draw a picture.

He is wearing a bowtie.

Han har på seg bowie.

The waiter is serving juice.

The waiter serverer juice.

Name

I Can...

- [ ] read the 1st sentence.
- [ ] read the 2nd sentence.
- [ ] make a sentence from a picture.
- [ ] color a picture.
- [ ] Draw a picture.

He has a suitcase.

Han har koffert.

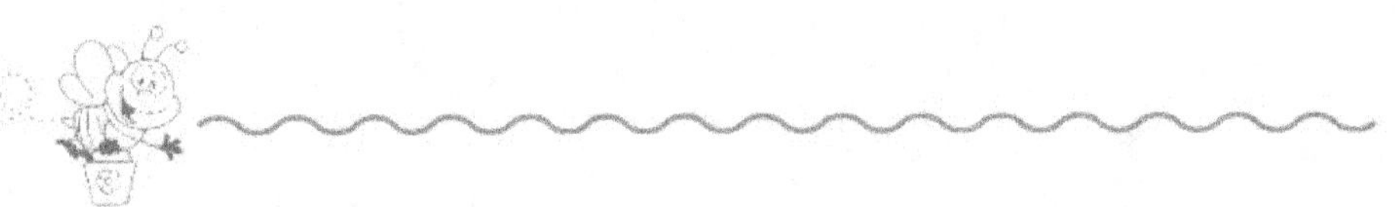

The engineer is holding a wrench.

Ingeniøren holder en skiftenøkkel.

Name _______________________ 

I Can...

- ☐ read the 1st sentence.
- ☐ read the 2nd sentence.
- ☐ make a sentence from a picture.
- ☐ color a picture.
- ☐ Draw a picture. 

The chef has a napkin.

Kokken har et serviett.

The chef serves delicious-looking food.

Kokken serverer deilig mat.

Name

I Can...

- [ ] read the 1st sentence.
- [ ] read the 2nd sentence.
- [ ] make a sentence from a picture.
- [ ] color a picture.
- [ ] Draw a picture.

The rooster has a big beak.

Hanen har et stort nebb.

The chicken is saying hello to us.

Kyllingen sier hei til oss.

Name

I Can...

- [ ] read the 1st sentence.
- [ ] read the 2nd sentence.
- [ ] make a sentence from a picture.
- [ ] color a picture.
- [ ] Draw a picture.

The bird is small.

Fuglen er liten.

The chick is on the telephone talking with his friend.

Kyllingen er på telefon og snakker med vennen sin.

Name

I Can...

- ☐ read the 1st sentence.
- ☐ read the 2nd sentence.
- ☐ make a sentence from a picture.
- ☐ color a picture.
- ☐ Draw a picture.

That is my ring.

Det er ringen min.

That is a beautiful ring.

Det er en vakker ring.

Name _______________

I Can...

- [ ] read the 1st sentence.
- [ ] read the 2nd sentence.
- [ ] make a sentence from a picture.
- [ ] color a picture.
- [ ] Draw a picture.

The duck has three eggs.

Anda har tre egg.

~~~~~~~~~~~~~~~~~~~~~~~~~~~~~~~

The duck has a big nose.

Anda har en stor nese.
~~~~~~~~~~~~~~~~~~~~~~~~~~~~~~~

Name

I Can...

- [ ] read the 1st sentence.
- [ ] read the 2nd sentence.
- [ ] make a sentence from a picture.
- [ ] color a picture.
- [ ] Draw a picture.

The swan is beautiful.

Svanen er vakker.

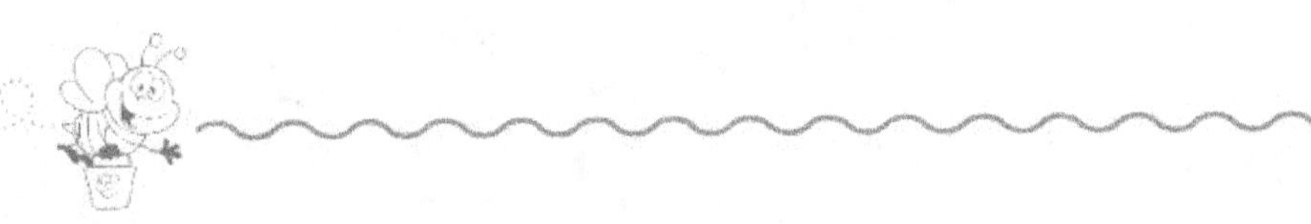

The graceful swan is striding through the water.

Den grasiøse svanen går gjennom vannet.

Name

I Can...

- [ ] read the 1st sentence.
- [ ] read the 2nd sentence.
- [ ] make a sentence from a picture.
- [ ] color a picture.
- [ ] Draw a picture.

The girl is wearing a dress.

Jenta har på seg en kjole.

The maid is cleaning our room.

Hushjelpen rengjør rommet vårt.

Name

I Can...

- [ ] read the 1st sentence.
- [ ] read the 2nd sentence.
- [ ] make a sentence from a picture.
- [ ] color a picture.
- [ ] Draw a picture.

The boy is running.

Gutten løper.

The little boy was running.

Den lille gutten løp.

Name ___________________ 

I Can...

- ☐ read the 1st sentence.
- ☐ read the 2nd sentence.
- ☐ make a sentence from a picture.
- ☐ color a picture.
- ☐ Draw a picture.

He is a musician.

Han er musiker.

He is playing a lively tune on his flute.

Han spiller en livlig melodi på fløyten sin.

Name ___________________________

I Can...

- [ ] read the 1st sentence.
- [ ] read the 2nd sentence.
- [ ] make a sentence from a picture.
- [ ] color a picture.
- [ ] Draw a picture.

He looks joyful.

Han ser glad ut.

 ~~~~~~~~~~~~~~~~~~~~~~~~~~~~~~~~~~~

That boy works in a band and plays the drum.

Den gutten jobber i et band og spiller trommelen.

Name

I Can...

- [ ] read the 1st sentence.
- [ ] read the 2nd sentence.
- [ ] make a sentence from a picture.
- [ ] color a picture.
- [ ] Draw a picture.

The dinosaur is a rock star.

Dinosauren er en rockestjerne.

The dragon is playing the guitar.

Dragen spiller gitar.

Name

I Can...

- [ ] read the 1st sentence.
- [ ] read the 2nd sentence.
- [ ] make a sentence from a picture.
- [ ] color a picture.
- [ ] Draw a picture.

The nurse helps the doctor.

Sykepleieren hjelper legen.

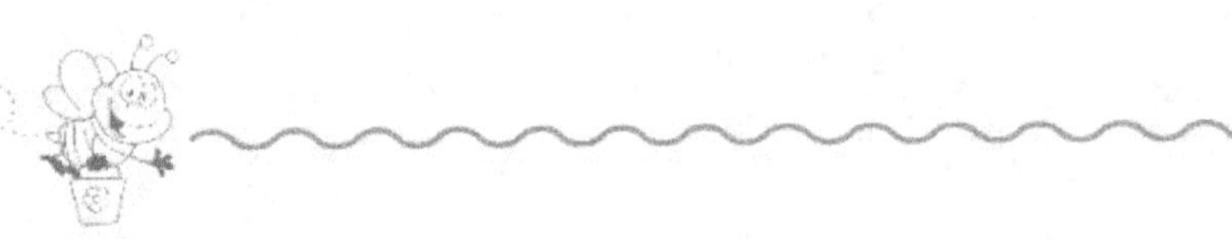

The nurse looks scary, holding a syringe.

Sykepleieren ser skummel ut og holder en sprøyte.

Name ___________________   44

I Can...

- [ ] read the 1st sentence.
- [ ] read the 2nd sentence.
- [ ] make a sentence from a picture.
- [ ] color a picture.
- [ ] Draw a picture.

She is wearing a crown.

Hun har på seg en krone.

 ~~~~~~~~~~~~~~~~~~~~~~~~~~~~~~~~~~~

The queen bee has a beautiful wand.

Dronningbien har en vakker stav.

Name

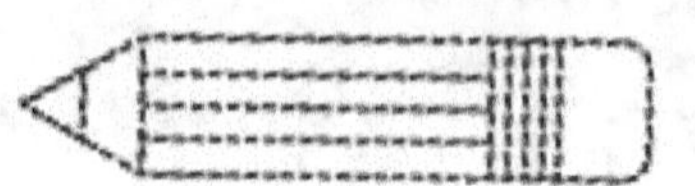

I Can...

- [ ] read the 1st sentence.
- [ ] read the 2nd sentence.
- [ ] make a sentence from a picture.
- [ ] color a picture.
- [ ] Draw a picture.

It is orange and black.

Den er oransje og svart.

The tiger is wearing a bow on its neck.

Tigeren har på seg en bue på nakken.

Name ___________________ 

I Can...

- [ ] read the 1st sentence.
- [ ] read the 2nd sentence.
- [ ] make a sentence from a picture.
- [ ] color a picture.
- [ ] Draw a picture.

The boy is carrying a lot of books.

Gutten har mange bøker på seg.

The boy is carrying so many books!

Gutten har med seg så mange bøker!

Name

I Can...

- [ ] read the 1st sentence.
- [ ] read the 2nd sentence.
- [ ] make a sentence from a picture.
- [ ] color a picture.
- [ ] Draw a picture.

The pizza looks delicious.

Pizzaen ser deilig ut.

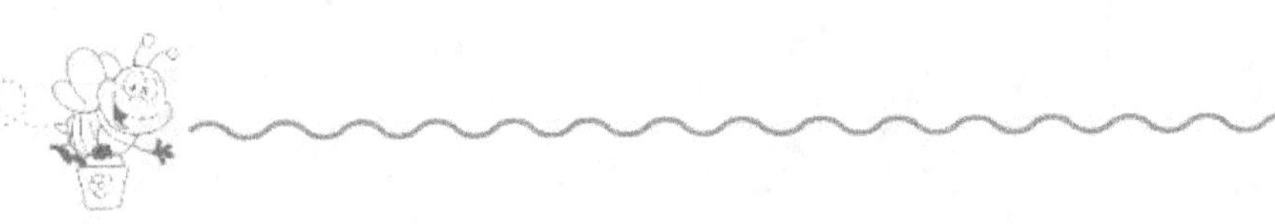

The waiter is serving steaming hot pizza.

The waiter serverer dampende varm pizza.

I Can...

- [ ] read the 1st sentence.
- [ ] read the 2nd sentence.
- [ ] make a sentence from a picture.
- [ ] color a picture.
- [ ] Draw a picture.

That is my dad's computer.

Det er datamaskinen til faren min.

 ~~~~~~~~~~~~~~~~~~~~~~~~~~~~

My dad works on the computer.

Faren min jobber på datamaskinen.

Name _______________

I Can...

- [ ] read the 1st sentence.
- [ ] read the 2nd sentence.
- [ ] make a sentence from a picture.
- [ ] color a picture.
- [ ] Draw a picture.

The farmer has a beard.

Bonden har skjegg.

~~~~~~

The gardener is going to plant flowers

Gartneren skal plante blomster
~~~~~~

Name ______________________

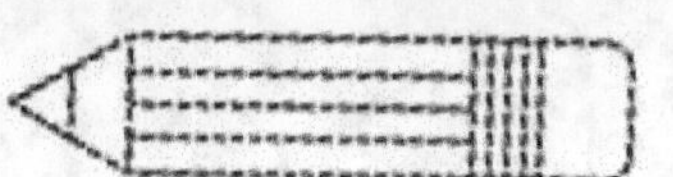

I Can...

- ☐ read the 1st sentence.
- ☐ read the 2nd sentence.
- ☐ make a sentence from a picture.
- ☐ color a picture.
- ☐ Draw a picture.

The strawberry is red.

Jordbæren er rød.

I love to drink strawberry juice.

Jeg elsker å drikke jordbær juice.

Name

I Can...

- [ ] read the 1st sentence.
- [ ] read the 2nd sentence.
- [ ] make a sentence from a picture.
- [ ] color a picture.
- [ ] Draw a picture.

The magician has a wand.

Trollmannen har en tryllestav.

The wizard likes to work with magic.

Veiviseren liker å jobbe med magi.

Name

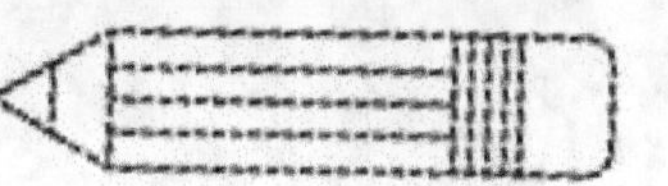

I Can...

- [ ] read the 1st sentence.
- [ ] read the 2nd sentence.
- [ ] make a sentence from a picture.
- [ ] color a picture.
- [ ] Draw a picture.

Reindeer has a scarf.

Reinsdyr har et skjerf.

Santa gave reindeer a big present.

Julenissen ga reinen en stor gave.

Name 

I Can...

- [ ] read the 1st sentence.
- [ ] read the 2nd sentence.
- [ ] make a sentence from a picture.
- [ ] color a picture.
- [ ] Draw a picture.

I have a lot of pencils.

Jeg har mange blyanter.

I have a lot of brushes and pencils.

Jeg har mye pensler og blyanter.

Name

I Can...

- [ ] read the 1st sentence.
- [ ] read the 2nd sentence.
- [ ] make a sentence from a picture.
- [ ] color a picture.
- [ ] Draw a picture.

Santa is fat.

Julenissen er feit.

Santa is having fun.

Julenissen har det gøy.

Name _______________________

I Can...

- ☐ read the 1st sentence.
- ☐ read the 2nd sentence.
- ☐ make a sentence from a picture.
- ☐ color a picture.
- ☐ Draw a picture.

I have one nose.

Jeg har en nese.

 ∼∼∼∼∼∼∼∼∼∼∼∼∼∼∼∼∼∼∼∼

The one is saying its name.

Den ene sier navnet sitt.

Name ___________

I Can...

- ☐ read the 1st sentence.
- ☐ read the 2nd sentence.
- ☐ make a sentence from a picture.
- ☐ color a picture.
- ☐ Draw a picture.

I have two ears.

Jeg har to ører.

The number "two" is holding up bunny ears.

Tallet "to" holder opp bunnyører.

Name

I Can...

- [ ] read the 1st sentence.
- [ ] read the 2nd sentence.
- [ ] make a sentence from a picture.
- [ ] color a picture.
- [ ] Draw a picture.

I have three buttons on my dress.

Jeg har tre knapper på kjolen.

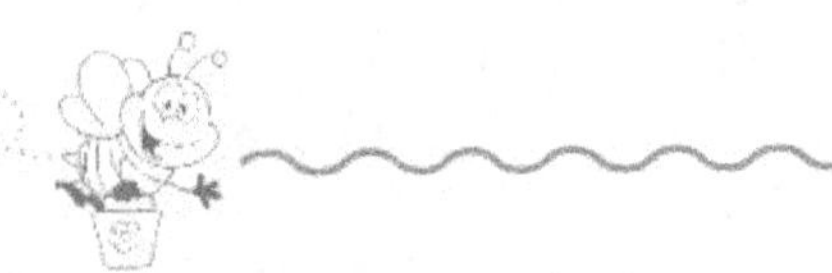

The number "three" is saying you got 3 out of 3.

Tallet "tre" sier at du fikk 3 av 3.

Name

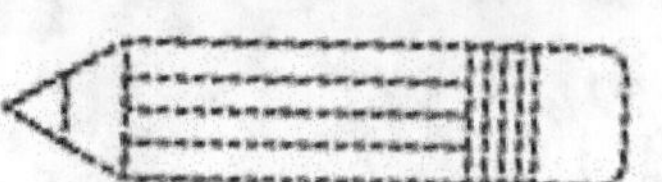

I Can...

- [ ] read the 1st sentence.
- [ ] read the 2nd sentence.
- [ ] make a sentence from a picture.
- [ ] color a picture.
- [ ] Draw a picture.

I have 0 tails.

Jeg har 0 haler.

The number "zero" is saying, Ok.

Tallet "null" sier: Ok.

Name

I Can...

- [ ] read the 1st sentence.
- [ ] read the 2nd sentence.
- [ ] make a sentence from a picture.
- [ ] color a picture.
- [ ] Draw a picture.

I have five fingers on 1 of my hands.

Jeg har fem fingre på 1 av hendene.

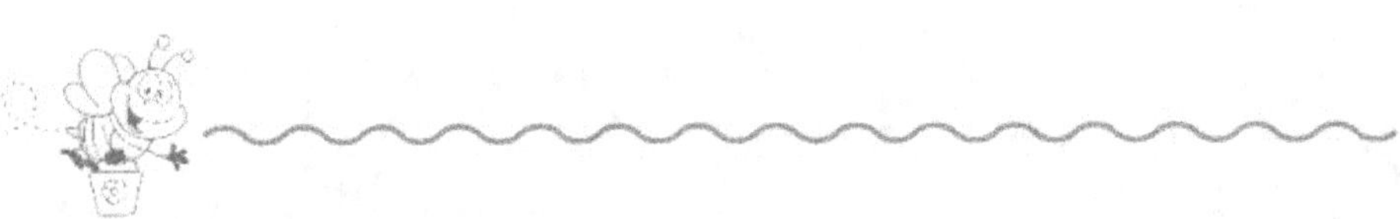

The number "five" is trying to give you a high five.

Tallet "fem" prøver å gi deg en høy fem.

Name

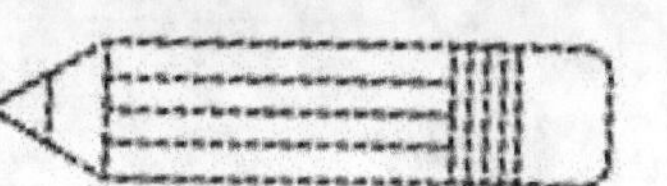

I Can...

- [ ] read the 1st sentence.
- [ ] read the 2nd sentence.
- [ ] make a sentence from a picture.
- [ ] color a picture.
- [ ] Draw a picture.

My cat has four legs.

Katten min har fire bein.

The number "four" is counting to four.

Tallet "fire" teller til fire.

Name

I Can...

- [ ] read the 1st sentence.
- [ ] read the 2nd sentence.
- [ ] make a sentence from a picture.
- [ ] color a picture.
- [ ] Draw a picture.

A butterfly has six legs.

En sommerfugl har seks ben.

The number "six" is saying 1+5=6.

Tallet "seks" sier 1 + 5 = 6.

Name _______________

I Can...

- [ ] read the 1st sentence.
- [ ] read the 2nd sentence.
- [ ] make a sentence from a picture.
- [ ] color a picture.
- [ ] Draw a picture.

A spider has eight legs.

En edderkopp har åtte ben.

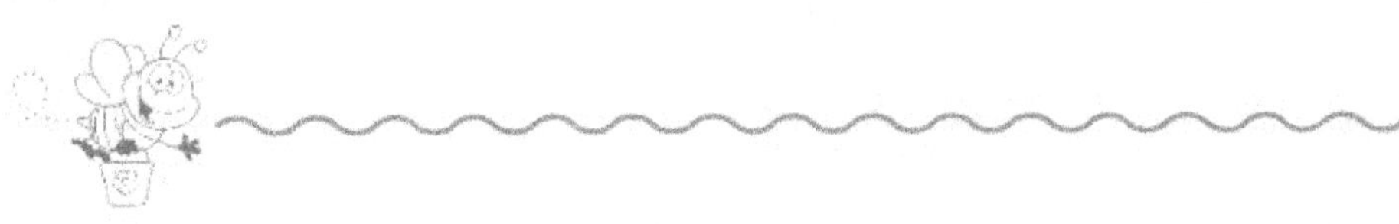

The happy and excited eight is holding up eight fingers

De glade og spente åtte holder på åtte fingre

Name

I Can...

- [ ] read the 1st sentence.
- [ ] read the 2nd sentence.
- [ ] make a sentence from a picture.
- [ ] color a picture.
- [ ] Draw a picture.

The rooster is going to wake people up.

Hanen skal vekke folk.

The rooster is on the fence.

Hanen er på gjerdet.

Name

I Can...

- [ ] read the 1st sentence.
- [ ] read the 2nd sentence.
- [ ] make a sentence from a picture.
- [ ] color a picture.
- [ ] Draw a picture.

My sister has nine stuffed animals.

Søsteren min har ni utstoppede dyr.

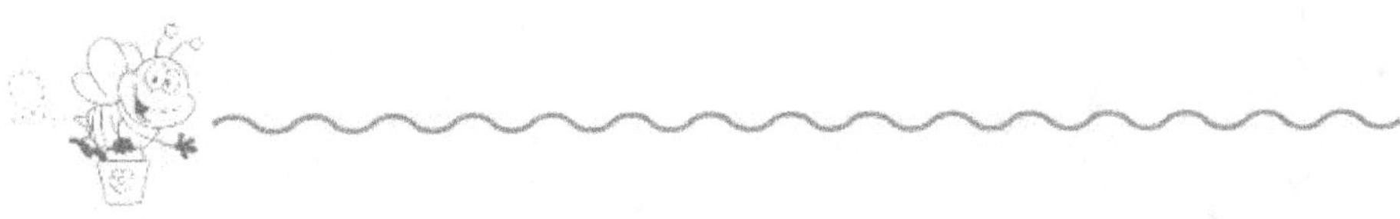

The smiling number nine is saying its name out loud.

Den smilende nummer ni sier navnet sitt høyt.

Name _______________ 

I Can...

- [ ] read the 1st sentence.
- [ ] read the 2nd sentence.
- [ ] make a sentence from a picture.
- [ ] color a picture.
- [ ] Draw a picture.

The baby bee has yellow and black stripes.

Babybien har gule og svarte striper.

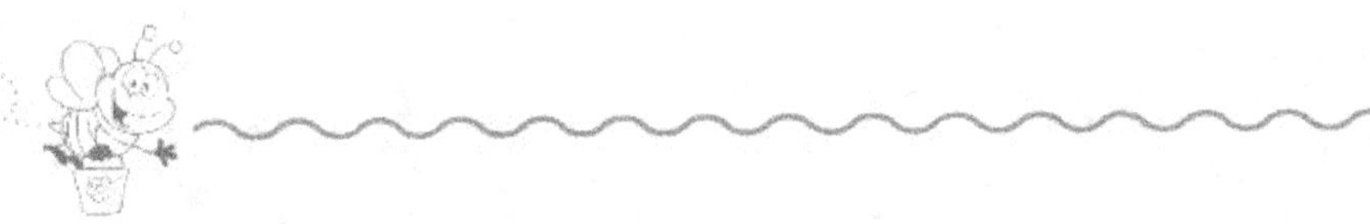

The bee is wearing a pink pacifier to calm itself.

Bien har på seg et rosa napp for å roe seg selv.

Name _______________________

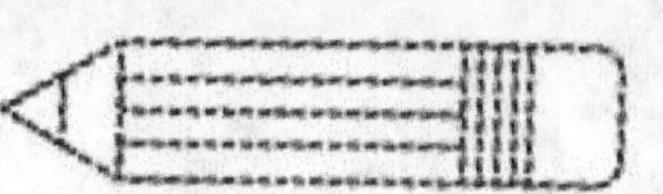

I Can...

- [ ] read the 1st sentence.
- [ ] read the 2nd sentence.
- [ ] make a sentence from a picture.
- [ ] color a picture.
- [ ] Draw a picture.

The ladybug has many spots.

Marihøna har mange flekker.

The red and black ladybug is just done eating some leaves.

Den røde og svarte marihøna er bare ferdig med å spise noen blader.

Name

I Can...

- [ ] read the 1st sentence.
- [ ] read the 2nd sentence.
- [ ] make a sentence from a picture.
- [ ] color a picture.
- [ ] Draw a picture.

The sheep are skinny.

Sauene er tynne.

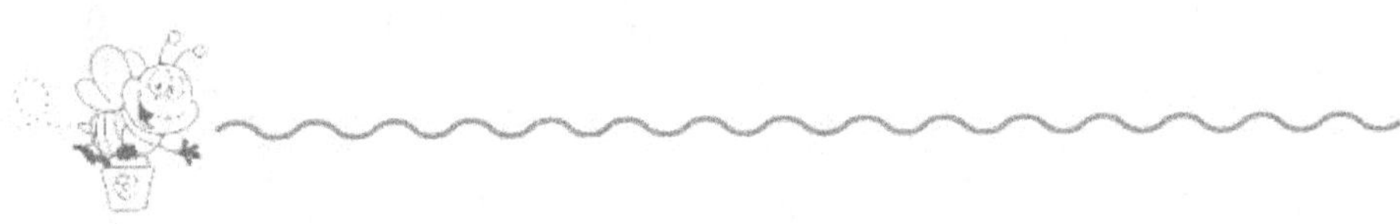

The white sheep have a lot of fluffy white wool to give away.

De hvite sauene har mye fluffy hvit ull å gi bort.

Name

I Can...

- [ ] read the 1st sentence.
- [ ] read the 2nd sentence.
- [ ] make a sentence from a picture.
- [ ] color a picture.
- [ ] Draw a picture.

The rabbit is entering an egg painting contest.

Kaninen deltar i en eggmalingskonkurranse.

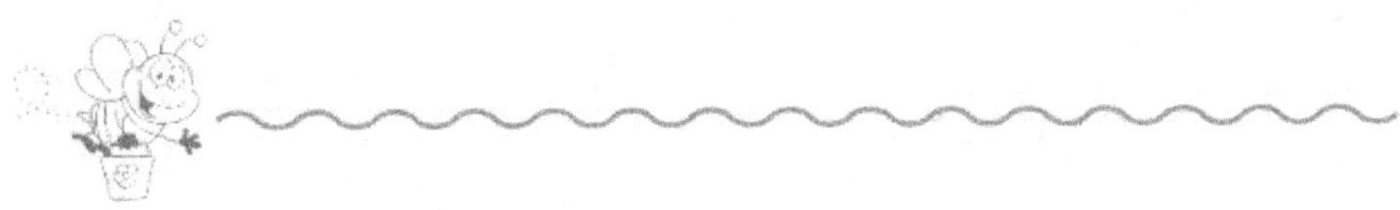

The Easter Bunny is painting a chocolate egg.

Påskeharen maler et sjokoladeegg.

Name 

I Can...

- [ ] read the 1st sentence.
- [ ] read the 2nd sentence.
- [ ] make a sentence from a picture.
- [ ] color a picture.
- [ ] Draw a picture.

The owl is a language arts teacher.

Uglen er en lærer i språkkunster.

An owl is teaching the kids in school about work.

En ugle lærer barna på skolen om jobb.

Name 

I Can...

- [ ] read the 1st sentence.
- [ ] read the 2nd sentence.
- [ ] make a sentence from a picture.
- [ ] color a picture.
- [ ] Draw a picture.

The man has an ancient hammer.

Mannen har en eldgammel hammer.

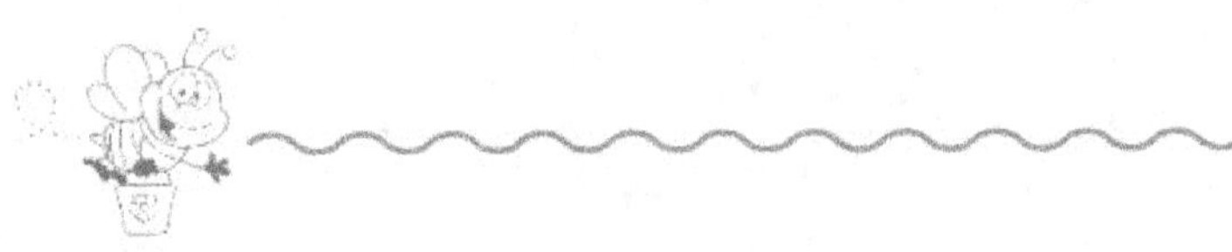

The builder man has gone to work on a project.

Byggmannen har gått på jobb med et prosjekt.

Name ____________

I Can...

- [ ] read the 1st sentence.
- [ ] read the 2nd sentence.
- [ ] make a sentence from a picture.
- [ ] color a picture.
- [ ] Draw a picture.

The goat has a friend.

Geiten har en venn.

 ~~~~~~~~~~~~~~~~~~~~~~~~~~~~~~

The old goat is proud of its golden bell.

Den gamle geiten er stolt av sin gullklokke.

Name

I Can...

- [ ] read the 1st sentence.
- [ ] read the 2nd sentence.
- [ ] make a sentence from a picture.
- [ ] color a picture.
- [ ] Draw a picture.

My mom's friend is a maid.

Min venns venn er en hushjelp.

The maid is going to clean the hotel room.

Hushjelpen kommer til å rengjøre hotellrommet.

Name

I Can...

- [ ] read the 1st sentence.
- [ ] read the 2nd sentence.
- [ ] make a sentence from a picture.
- [ ] color a picture.
- [ ] Draw a picture.

I went to the zoo.

Jeg dro til dyrehagen.

The animals are having a big celebration.

Dyrene holder en stor feiring.

Name

I Can...

- [ ] read the 1st sentence.
- [ ] read the 2nd sentence.
- [ ] make a sentence from a picture.
- [ ] color a picture.
- [ ] Draw a picture.

The dinosaur has a pillow.

Dinosauren har en pute.

The dragon is using the rock to build its house.

Dragen bruker steinen til å bygge huset sitt.

Name

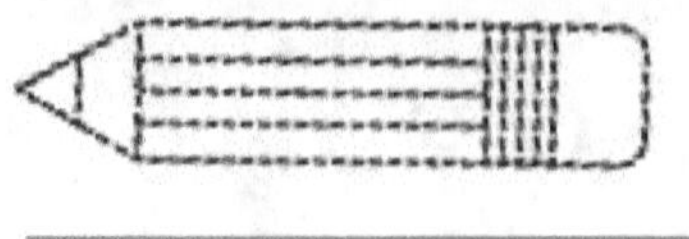

I Can...

- [ ] read the 1st sentence.
- [ ] read the 2nd sentence.
- [ ] make a sentence from a picture.
- [ ] color a picture.
- [ ] Draw a picture.

The boy is excited to go to school.

Gutten er spent på å gå på skolen.

The boy is late for school, so he is sprinting.

Gutten er sent på skolen, så han snurrer.

Name

I Can...

- [ ] read the 1st sentence.
- [ ] read the 2nd sentence.
- [ ] make a sentence from a picture.
- [ ] color a picture.
- [ ] Draw a picture.

The kids on the school bus are going to school.

Barna på skolebussen skal på skolen.

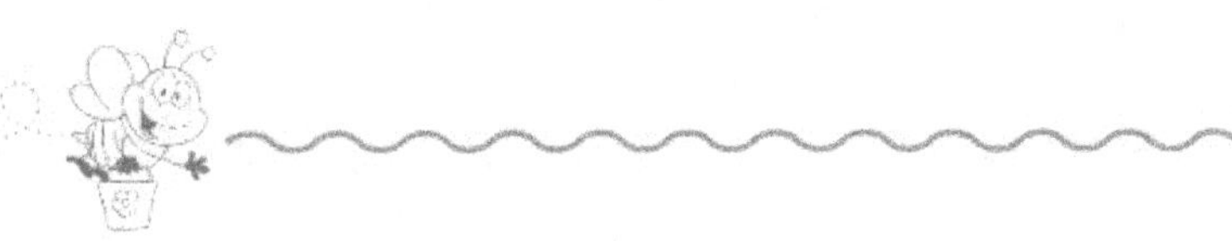

The children are going on a field trip on the yellow bus.

Barna skal på felttur på den gule bussen.

Name ______________________

I Can...

- [ ] read the 1st sentence.
- [ ] read the 2nd sentence.
- [ ] make a sentence from a picture.
- [ ] color a picture.
- [ ] Draw a picture.

The cobra is very lovely.

Kobraen er veldig deilig.

The rattlesnake is looking for its dinner.

Klapperslangen leter etter middagen.

Name 

I Can...

- [ ] read the 1st sentence.
- [ ] read the 2nd sentence.
- [ ] make a sentence from a picture.
- [ ] color a picture.
- [ ] Draw a picture.

That is a fat dog!

Det er en feit hund!

~~~~~~~~~~~~~~~~~~~~~~~~~~~~~

This dog is wagging its tail for more treats.

Denne hunden satser på halen for flere godbiter.
~~~~~~~~~~~~~~~~~~~~~~~~~~~~~

Name

I Can...

- [ ] read the 1st sentence.
- [ ] read the 2nd sentence.
- [ ] make a sentence from a picture.
- [ ] color a picture.
- [ ] Draw a picture.

The elephant lives in the zoo.

Elefanten bor i dyrehagen.

The elephant has a long trunk to spray water.

Elefanten har en lang koffert for å spraye vann.

Name ___________

I Can...

- ☐ read the 1st sentence.
- ☐ read the 2nd sentence.
- ☐ make a sentence from a picture.
- ☐ color a picture.
- ☐ Draw a picture.

The giraffe eats vegetables.

Sjiraffen spiser grønnsaker.

The giraffe has an extremely long neck.

Sjiraffen har en ekstremt lang nakke.

Name ____________________

I Can...

- [ ] read the 1st sentence.
- [ ] read the 2nd sentence.
- [ ] make a sentence from a picture.
- [ ] color a picture.
- [ ] Draw a picture.

The chipmunk has a soft tummy.

Chipmunk har en myk mage.

 ～～～～～～～～～～～～～～

The Chipmunk is about to eat a brown acorn.

Chipmunk er i ferd med å spise en brun eikenøtt.

Name

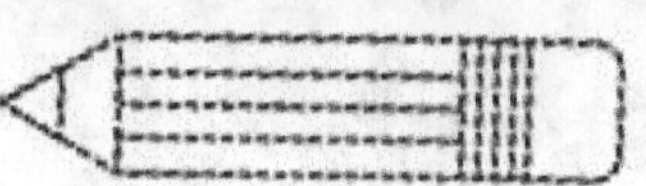

I Can...

- [ ] read the 1st sentence.
- [ ] read the 2nd sentence.
- [ ] make a sentence from a picture.
- [ ] color a picture.
- [ ] Draw a picture.

I have ten toes in total.

Jeg har ti tær totalt.

The one and the zero are holding hands.

Den og nullen holder hender.

Name

I Can...

- [ ] read the 1st sentence.
- [ ] read the 2nd sentence.
- [ ] make a sentence from a picture.
- [ ] color a picture.
- [ ] Draw a picture.

The alligator is jumping.

Alligatoren hopper.

The crocodile is excited.

Krokodillen er spent.

Name ___________________________ 

I Can...

- [ ] read the 1st sentence.
- [ ] read the 2nd sentence.
- [ ] make a sentence from a picture.
- [ ] color a picture.
- [ ] Draw a picture.

I found an ant.

Jeg fant en maur.

 ~~~~~~

The ant is telling a story.

Myren forteller en historie.

Name

I Can...

- [ ] read the 1st sentence.
- [ ] read the 2nd sentence.
- [ ] make a sentence from a picture.
- [ ] color a picture.
- [ ] Draw a picture.

The bat sleeps upside down.

Flaggermusen sover opp ned.

The bat is ready to fly.

Flaggermusen er klar til å fly.

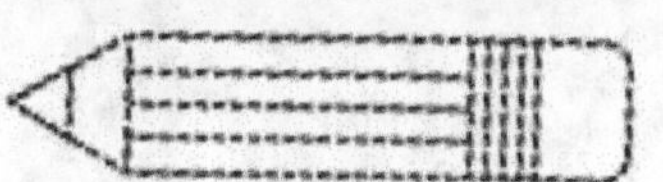

I Can...

- [ ] read the 1st sentence.
- [ ] read the 2nd sentence.
- [ ] make a sentence from a picture.
- [ ] color a picture.
- [ ] Draw a picture.

The cat is very tired.

Katten er veldig sliten.

The cat is taking a nap.

Katten tar en lur.

Name

I Can...

- [ ] read the 1st sentence.
- [ ] read the 2nd sentence.
- [ ] make a sentence from a picture.
- [ ] color a picture.
- [ ] Draw a picture.

The dog likes to play.

Hunden liker å leke.

The dog is playing with a bone.

Hunden leker med et bein.

Name

I Can...

- [ ] read the 1st sentence.
- [ ] read the 2nd sentence.
- [ ] make a sentence from a picture.
- [ ] color a picture.
- [ ] Draw a picture.

The elephant has eyelashes.

Elefanten har øyevipper.

The elephant is shy.

Elefanten er sjenert.

Name

I Can...

- [ ] read the 1st sentence.
- [ ] read the 2nd sentence.
- [ ] make a sentence from a picture.
- [ ] color a picture.
- [ ] Draw a picture.

The frog is hopping.

Frosken hopper.

The frog is trying to catch the fly.

Frosken prøver å fange flua.

Name

I Can...

- [ ] read the 1st sentence.
- [ ] read the 2nd sentence.
- [ ] make a sentence from a picture.
- [ ] color a picture.
- [ ] Draw a picture.

The goat is sleepily walking around.

Geita går søvnig rundt.

The goat is eating grass.

Geiten spiser gress.

Name ___________________ 

I Can...

- [ ] read the 1st sentence.
- [ ] read the 2nd sentence.
- [ ] make a sentence from a picture.
- [ ] color a picture.
- [ ] Draw a picture.

The hippo has a big head.

Flodhesten har et stort hode.

The hippo has a big head.

Flodhesten har et stort hode.

Name

I Can...

- ☐ read the 1st sentence.
- ☐ read the 2nd sentence.
- ☐ make a sentence from a picture.
- ☐ color a picture.
- ☐ Draw a picture.

The iguana has a long tail.

Leguanen har en lang hale.

The iguana is hiding behind the letter I.

Leguanen gjemmer seg bak bokstaven I.

Name 

I Can...

- [ ] read the 1st sentence.
- [ ] read the 2nd sentence.
- [ ] make a sentence from a picture.
- [ ] color a picture.
- [ ] Draw a picture.

Mom bought a new bottle of jam.

Mamma kjøpte en ny flaske syltetøy.

There is jam on the bread.

Det er syltetøy på brødet.

Name

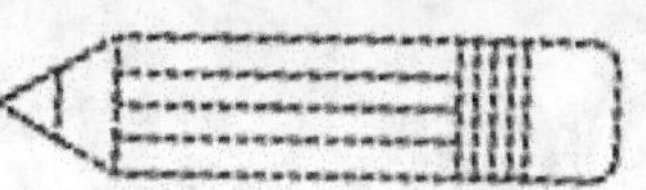

I Can...

- [ ] read the 1st sentence.
- [ ] read the 2nd sentence.
- [ ] make a sentence from a picture.
- [ ] color a picture.
- [ ] Draw a picture.

The kite has a beautiful tail.

Kiten har en vakker hale.

The kite is on the ground.

Kiten er på bakken.

Name _______________________

I Can...

- [ ] read the 1st sentence.
- [ ] read the 2nd sentence.
- [ ] make a sentence from a picture.
- [ ] color a picture.
- [ ] Draw a picture.

The lion is timid.

Løven er redd.

____

The lion is big.

Løven er stor.

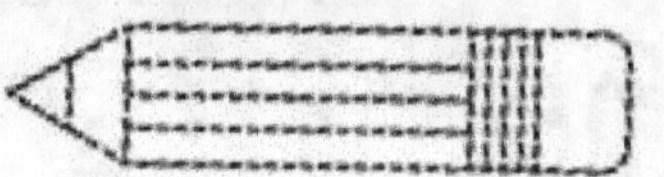

I Can...

- [ ] read the 1st sentence.
- [ ] read the 2nd sentence.
- [ ] make a sentence from a picture.
- [ ] color a picture.
- [ ] Draw a picture.

I like mice.

Jeg liker mus.

A rat is on top of the letter M

En rotte er på toppen av bokstaven M

Name

I Can...

- [ ] read the 1st sentence.
- [ ] read the 2nd sentence.
- [ ] make a sentence from a picture.
- [ ] color a picture.
- [ ] Draw a picture.

The nose is breathing.

Nesen puster.

The letter N stands for a nose.

Bokstaven N står for en nese.

Name

I Can...

- [ ] read the 1st sentence.
- [ ] read the 2nd sentence.
- [ ] make a sentence from a picture.
- [ ] color a picture.
- [ ] Draw a picture.

The octopus lives underwater.

Blekkspruten lever under vann.

The octopus has eight tentacles.

Blekkspruten har åtte tentakler.

Name

I Can...

- [ ] read the 1st sentence.
- [ ] read the 2nd sentence.
- [ ] make a sentence from a picture.
- [ ] color a picture.
- [ ] Draw a picture.

The penguin eats fish.

Pingvinen spiser fisk.

The penguin lives in the arctic.

Pingvinen lever i det arktiske.

Name

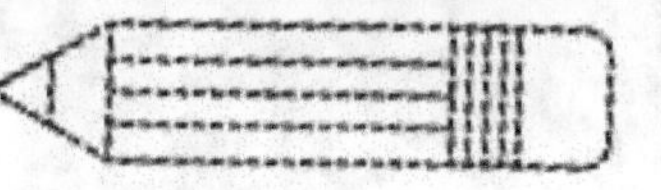

I Can...

- [ ] read the 1st sentence.
- [ ] read the 2nd sentence.
- [ ] make a sentence from a picture.
- [ ] color a picture.
- [ ] Draw a picture.

The queen has a wand.

Dronningen har en tryllestav.

The queen is beautiful.

Dronningen er vakker.

Name

I Can...

- [ ] read the 1st sentence.
- [ ] read the 2nd sentence.
- [ ] make a sentence from a picture.
- [ ] color a picture.
- [ ] Draw a picture.

The rabbit has long ears.

Kaninen har lange ører.

The rabbit is thinking about something.

Kaninen tenker på noe.

Name _______________________________ 

I Can...

- [ ] read the 1st sentence.
- [ ] read the 2nd sentence.
- [ ] make a sentence from a picture.
- [ ] color a picture.
- [ ] Draw a picture.

The snake has polka dots.

Slangen har prikker.

~~~~~~~~~~~~~~~~~~~~~~~~~~~~~~~~~~~~~

The snake is licking its lip because it is hungry.

Slangen slikker leppa fordi den er sulten.
~~~~~~~~~~~~~~~~~~~~~~~~~~~~~~~~~~~~~

Name

I Can...

- [ ] read the 1st sentence.
- [ ] read the 2nd sentence.
- [ ] make a sentence from a picture.
- [ ] color a picture.
- [ ] Draw a picture.

The tortoise has a pointy shell.

Skilpadden har et spisse skall.

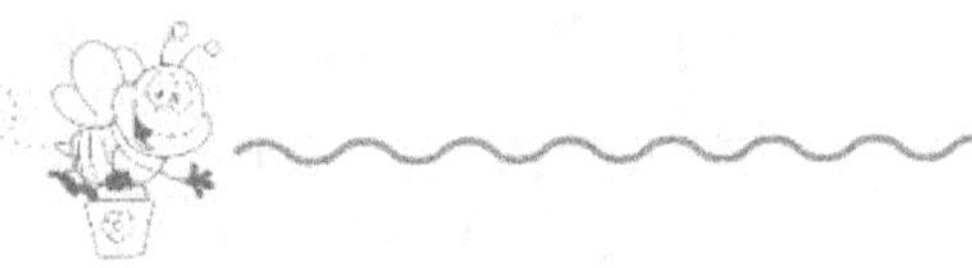

The turtle has a robust shell but is very slow.

Skilpadden har et robust skall, men er veldig treg.

Name _______________________

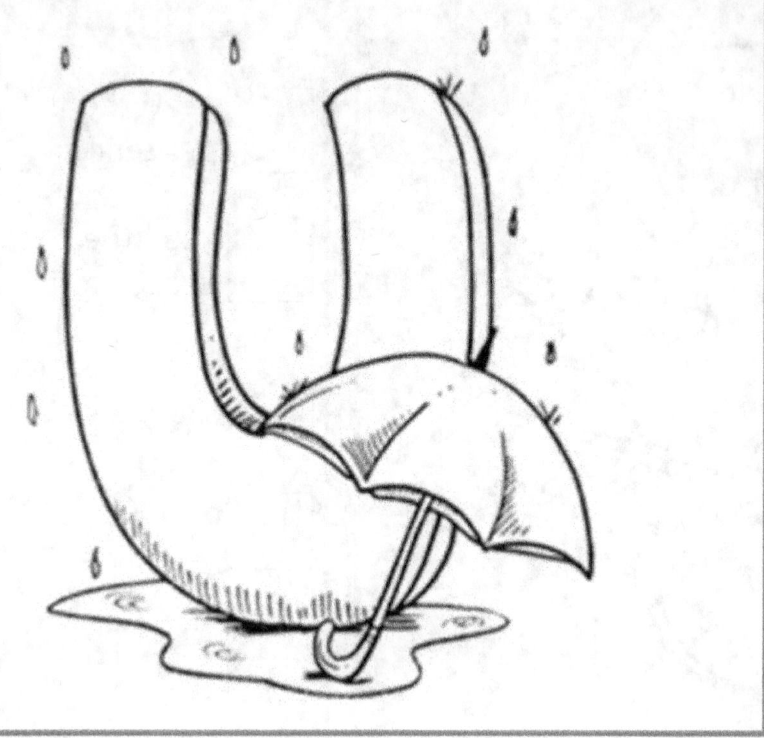

I Can...

- [ ] read the 1st sentence.
- [ ] read the 2nd sentence.
- [ ] make a sentence from a picture.
- [ ] color a picture.
- [ ] Draw a picture.

It's raining.

Det regner.

We use the umbrella when it's raining.

Vi bruker paraplyen når det regner.

Name

I Can...

- [ ] read the 1st sentence.
- [ ] read the 2nd sentence.
- [ ] make a sentence from a picture.
- [ ] color a picture.
- [ ] Draw a picture.

The violin is a musical instrument.

Fiolinen er et musikkinstrument.

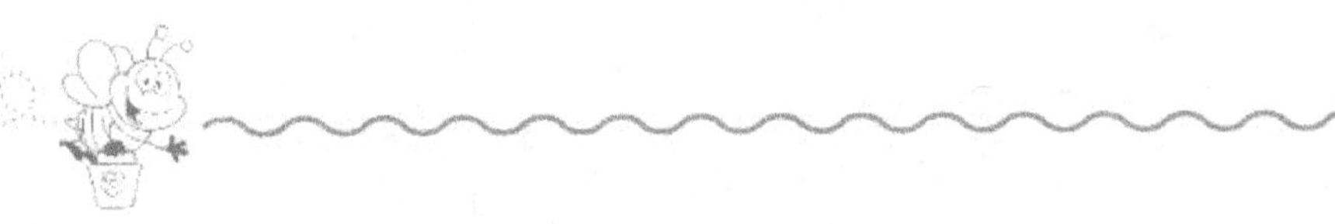

A violin can play beautiful music if played correctly.

En fiolin kan spille vakker musikk hvis den spilles riktig.

I Can...

- [ ] read the 1st sentence.
- [ ] read the 2nd sentence.
- [ ] make a sentence from a picture.
- [ ] color a picture.
- [ ] Draw a picture.

The walrus has a friend.

Hvalrossen har en venn.

The walrus has unusually sharp teeth.

Hvalrossen har uvanlig skarpe tenner.

Name

I Can...

- [ ] read the 1st sentence.
- [ ] read the 2nd sentence.
- [ ] make a sentence from a picture.
- [ ] color a picture.
- [ ] Draw a picture.

The xylophone is a colorful instrument.

Xylofonen er et fargerikt instrument.

The xylophone is an instrument like the piano.

Xylofonen er et instrument som piano.

Name

I Can...

- [ ] read the 1st sentence.
- [ ] read the 2nd sentence.
- [ ] make a sentence from a picture.
- [ ] color a picture.
- [ ] Draw a picture.

The boy has a little hat.

Gutten har en liten hatt.

The boy is having fun playing with a yoyo.

Gutten har det gøy å leke med en yoyo.

I Can...

- [ ] read the 1st sentence.
- [ ] read the 2nd sentence.
- [ ] make a sentence from a picture.
- [ ] color a picture.
- [ ] Draw a picture.

The zebra has a tail.

Sebraen har en hale.

The zebra has black and white stripes.

Sebraen har svarte og hvite striper.

Name _______________________ 

I Can...

- [ ] read the 1st sentence.
- [ ] read the 2nd sentence.
- [ ] make a sentence from a picture.
- [ ] color a picture.
- [ ] Draw a picture.

I have a candle on my cake.

Jeg har et lys på kaken.

 ﹏﹏﹏﹏﹏﹏﹏﹏﹏﹏﹏﹏

I had a small birthday cake for my party.

Jeg hadde en liten bursdagskake til festen min.

Name

I Can...

- [ ] read the 1st sentence.
- [ ] read the 2nd sentence.
- [ ] make a sentence from a picture.
- [ ] color a picture.
- [ ] Draw a picture.

The astronaut is going on a mission.

Astronauten skal på oppdrag.

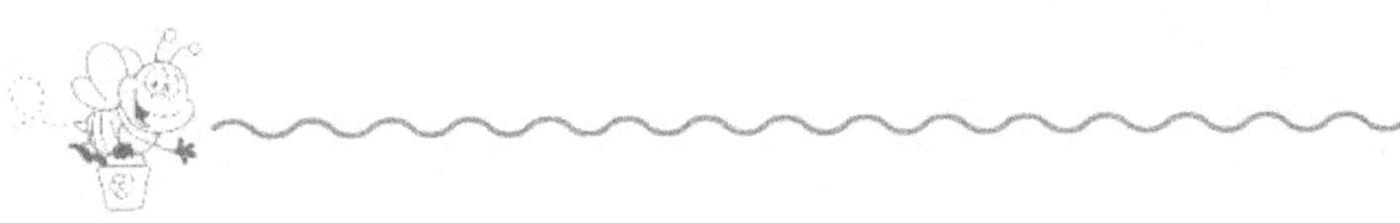

An astronaut has to explore our universe so that we would have more knowledge.

En astronaut må utforske universet vårt slik at vi vil ha mer kunnskap.

Name

I Can...

- [ ] read the 1st sentence.
- [ ] read the 2nd sentence.
- [ ] make a sentence from a picture.
- [ ] color a picture.
- [ ] Draw a picture.

The samurai is going for a morning jog.

Samurai skal på morgenjoggetur.

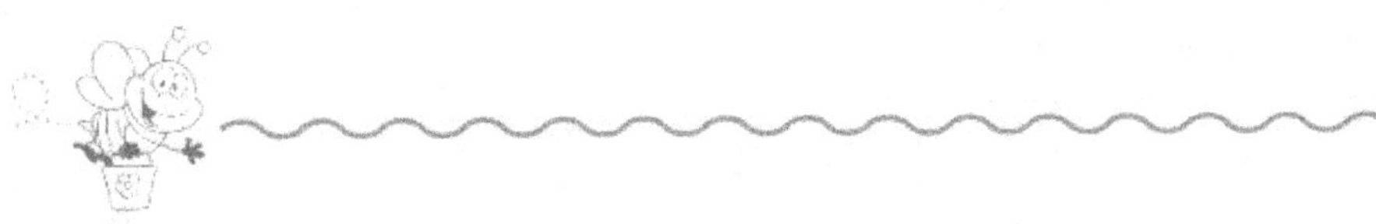

The samurai is training to become good at fighting.

Samuraiene trener for å bli gode til å kjempe.

Name

I Can...

- [ ] read the 1st sentence.
- [ ] read the 2nd sentence.
- [ ] make a sentence from a picture.
- [ ] color a picture.
- [ ] Draw a picture.

My friend is having a gigantic cake.

Venninnen min har en gigantisk kake.

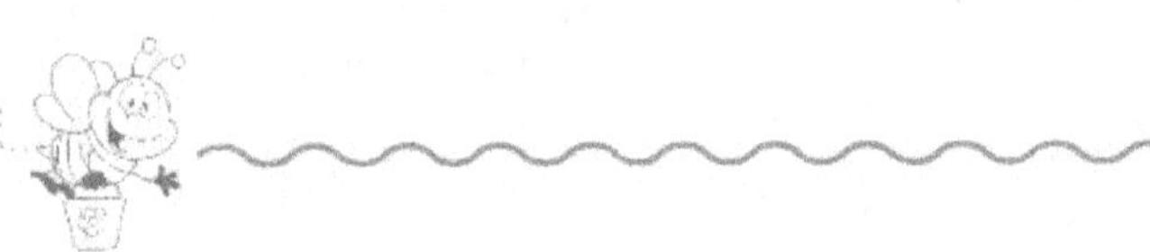

I had a humongous birthday cake for my celebration.

Jeg hadde en humoristisk bursdagskake til feiringen min.

Name _______________________

I Can...

- [ ] read the 1st sentence.
- [ ] read the 2nd sentence.
- [ ] make a sentence from a picture.
- [ ] color a picture.
- [ ] Draw a picture.

The frog is chasing the fly.

Frosken jager flua.

 ~~~~~~~~~~~~~~~~~~~~~~~~~~~~~~~~~~~~~~

The green frog is trying to catch the fly.

Den grønne frosken prøver å fange flua.

Name 

I Can...

- [ ] read the 1st sentence.
- [ ] read the 2nd sentence.
- [ ] make a sentence from a picture.
- [ ] color a picture.
- [ ] Draw a picture.

The ladybug has six legs.

Marihøna har seks bein.

The ladybug is on the leaf.

Marihøna er på bladet.

Name ____________________

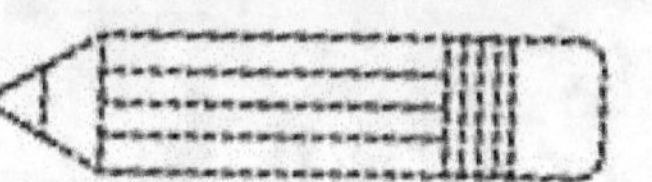

I Can...

- [ ] read the 1st sentence.
- [ ] read the 2nd sentence.
- [ ] make a sentence from a picture.
- [ ] color a picture.
- [ ] Draw a picture.

The dragon is sick.

Dragen er syk.

The dragon just ate something spicy, so he needed water.

Dragen bare spiste noe krydret, så han trengte vann.

Name _______________

I Can...

☐ read the 1st sentence.

☐ read the 2nd sentence.

☐ make a sentence from a picture.

☐ color a picture.

☐ Draw a picture.

That is a baby cow.

Det er en baby-ku.

A little cow is walking around near the barn.

En liten ku går rundt i låven.

Name

I Can...

- [ ] read the 1st sentence.
- [ ] read the 2nd sentence.
- [ ] make a sentence from a picture.
- [ ] color a picture.
- [ ] Draw a picture.

The frog has a big smile.

Frosken har et stort smil.

The frog is smiling because it is happy.

Frosken smiler fordi den er glad.

Name

I Can...

- [ ] read the 1st sentence.
- [ ] read the 2nd sentence.
- [ ] make a sentence from a picture.
- [ ] color a picture.
- [ ] Draw a picture.

The frog has a big mouth.

Frosken har en stor munn.

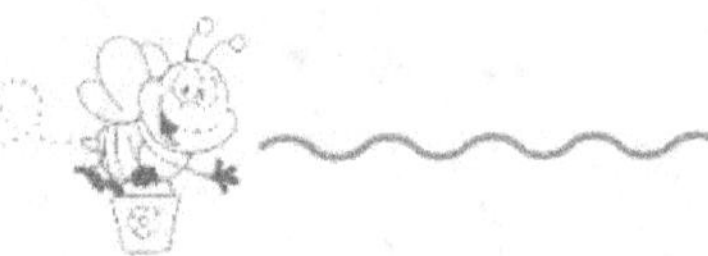

The frog is waving to us.

Frosken vinker til oss.